Stereophonics
The Hit Singles

Published by:
Wise Publications 8/9 Frith Street, London W1D 3JB, England.

Exclusive distributors:
Music Sales Limited Distribution Centre, Newmarket Road, Bury St. Edmunds, Suffolk IP33 3YB, England.
Music Sales Pty Limited 120 Rothschild Avenue, Rosebery, NSW 2018, Australia.

Order No. AM975931
ISBN 0-7119-9748-9
This book © Copyright 2003 by Wise Publications.

Compiled by Nick Crispin.
Music engraved by Paul Ewers Music Design.
Photographs courtesy of London Features International.
Printed in the United Kingdom.

Your Guarantee of Quality:
As publishers, we strive to produce every book to the highest commercial standards.
This book has been carefully designed to minimise awkward page turns and to make playing from it a real pleasure.
Particular care has been given to specifying acid-free, neutral-sized paper made from pulps which have not been elemental chlorine bleached.
This pulp is from farmed sustainable forests and was produced with special regard for the environment.
Throughout, the printing and binding have been planned to ensure a sturdy, attractive publication which should give years of enjoyment.
If your copy fails to meet our high standards, please inform us and we will gladly replace it.

www.musicsales.com

This publication is not authorised for sale in
the United States of America and/or Canada

Wise Publications
part of The Music Sales Group

London / New York / Paris / Sydney / Copenhagen / Berlin / Madrid / Tokyo

Have A Nice Day

Words & Music by Kelly Jones

Ba ba da ba ba ba da da. Ba ba da ba ba ba da da.

Ba ba da ba ba ba da da. Ba ba da ba ba ba da da.

1. San Fran-cis-co Bay past pier thir-ty nine. Ear-ly P. M. can't

re-mem-ber what time.— Got the wait-ing cab, stopped at the red light.

Add-ress un-sure of, but it turned out just right.

2. It start-ed straight off "Com - ing here is hell." That's his first words,
(Verses 3 & 4 see block lyrics)

we asked what he meant.— He said "And where ya from?" We told him our lot,

"When ya take a ho-li-day, is this what you want?"

So have a nice—

Ba ba da ba ba ba da ba. Ba ba da ba ba ba da ba.
day.— Have a nice— day.— Have a nice—

Ba ba da ba ba ba da ba. Ba ba da ba ba ba da ba.
day._____ Have a nice_____ day._____

Oh._____

Freetime

a tempo

D.%. al Coda

Ba ba da ba ba ba da ba. Ba ba da ba ba ba da ba.

6

Verse 3:

Lie around all day
Have a drink to chase
Yourself and tourists,
Yeah, that's what I hate
You say we're going wrong
We've all become the same
We dress the same ways
Only our accents change.

So have a nice day *etc.*

Verse 4:

Swim in the ocean
That be my dish
I'll drive around all day
And kill processed fish
It's all money gum
No artists anymore
You're only in it now
To make more, more, more.

So have a nice day *etc.*

Handbags And Gladrags

Words & Music by Michael D'Abo

Cor Anglais

Con pedale

1. Ev - er see a blind man cross the road___ try'n to make the oth - er side?_
(Verse 2 see block lyric)

Ev-er see a young girl grow-in' old,

try'n to make her-self a bride?

So what be-comes of you my love,

when they've fin-'lly stripped you of the hand-bags and the glad-rags that your poor old gran - dad had to sweat to buy___ you.

Cor Anglais

Yeah, ___ yeah.___

3. Sing a song of six - pence for your sake___ and drink a bot - tle full of___

rye.

Four and twen-ty black birds in a cake and bake them all in a pie.

They told me you missed school to-day, so what I sug-gest you just throw them all a-way. The

11

hand - bags and the glad - rags that your poor__ old gran - dad had to sweat__ to buy.__

Oh._____

you.

Verse 2 :
Once I was a young man
And all I thought I had to do was smile
Well, you are still a young girl
And you've bought everything in style.

So once you think you're in you're in, you're out.
'Cause you don't mean a single thing without
The handbags and the gladrags *etc.*

I Wouldn't Believe Your Radio

Words by Kelly Jones
Music by Kelly Jones, Richard Jones & Stuart Cable

14

tun - nel un - der-sea,___ you nev - er know, if it

cracks in half,___ you're nev-er ev-er gon - na see me.___

But you can have it all if you like.___

You can have it all if you like,___ and you can pay for it the rest of your___

Aadd9
Cmaj7
G6
li - - - - i - i - i - ife.
3
Aadd9
Cmaj7
G6
Li - - - - - - i - i - i - ife.
3
D
C
G
Guitar
D
C
G

Life in the sum - mer's on it's back,— you'd have to a - gree—

— that that's the crack,— so take what you want,— I'm not com - ing

back._____ So you can have it

all if you like.___

You can have it all if you like.—

Oh you can have it all if you like.—

You can have it

all if you like,— and you can pay for it the rest of your—

18

Verse 2:
I wouldn't believe your wireless radio
If I had myself a flying giraffe
You'd have one in a box with a window.

But you can have it all *etc.*

Maybe Tomorrow

Words & Music by Kelly Jones

Ooh, bap a ooh,

Ooh, bap a ooh,

Ooh, bap a ooh,

Ooh, bap a ooh,

1. I've been down and I'm won-de-ring why these lit-tle black clouds keep-a walk-ing a-round with

2. I look a-round at a beau-ti-ful life I've been the up-per side of down, been the in-side of out but we

Gm Fadd9 E♭maj7

me,   with me.___   It wastes time and I'd rath-er be high___ I think I'll
breathe, we breathe.___   I wan-na breeze and an op-en___ mind,_ I wan-na

Cm7   Gm

walk me out-side and buy a rain-bow smile_ but be free,___   they're all___
swim in the o-cean, wan-na take my time_ for me,___   all___

Fadd9 E♭maj7 Cm7

free.___
me.___   So may-be to-mor-row   I'll find my

Gm7 F6 E♭maj7

way_____ home.___   So may-be___ to-mor-

21

- row,　　I'll find my way_____ home.___

home.___

Ah,　　　　　ah,

Ooh,　　ooh,___　　ooh,　　ooh,___

ah._____

ooh,　　　ooh,___　　ooh,　　　ooh.___

Ah,

Ooh,　　　ooh,___

D7
Gm7
3fr
ah.
ooh,
ooh,
ah,
ooh,
ooh.
Fadd9
G5
3fr
ah.
Ooh,
ooh,
E♭maj7
ooh,
ooh,
Cm7
3fr
Gm
3fr

So may - be to - mor - row I'll find my

way_____ home._____

So may - be_____ to - mor - row, I'll find my

way_____ home._____

Vocal ad lib.

24

Na, na, na, na. Na, na, na, na. Na, na, na,

na. Na, na, na, na.___ Na, na, na, na_____ oh.___

Oh,_____ oh, ah oh.

Traffic

Words by Kelly Jones
Music by Kelly Jones, Richard Jones & Stuart Cable

1. We all face the same
way, still it takes all day; I take a look to my
(Verses 2 & 3 see block lyrics)

left,   pick out the worst and the_____ best._____   She paints__ her lip.__

grea-sy and__ thick;   an-oth-er mir-ror stare,__   and she's go-ing

1.

2, 3.

where?_____   2. An-oth-er of-fice af - fair, _____   Is__

a - ny - one____ go - ing   a - ny - where?__   Ev-'ry-one____ got-ta be _____ some - where. _____

To Coda ⊕

D.%. al Coda
(as 2nd time)

3. She got a bo - dy in the

⊕ Coda

28

F add9 F F add9 F C
Wait ta - bles for a
C F
crook who wrote a hard - back book. D'you teach kids how to
Am F
read, or sell your bo - dy on their street? A nurse with - out
C Am
a job? An-oth - er up - town snob? But have I got you all

wrong?   One look and you were_____ go - - ne._____   Is_____

1, 2.
a - ny - one_____   go - ing_____   a - ny - where?_____   Is_____

3.
a - ny - where?_____   Ev - 'ry - one_____

got - ta   be_____   some - where._____

Verse 2:

Another office affair, to kill an unborn scare
You talk dirty to a priest, it makes them human at least
But is she running away to start a brand new day?
Or's she going home? Why's she driving alone?

Is anyone going anywhere *etc.*

Verse 3:

She got a body in the boot, or just bags full of food?
Those are model's legs; but are they women's, are they men's?
She shouts down the phone, missed a payment on the loan
She gotta be above the rest, keeping up with the best.

Is anyone going anythere *etc.*